ChordTime®

O

Christmas

Level 2B

I-IV-V⁷ chords in keys
of C, G and F

I-IV-V^7 chords in keys of C, G and F

This book belongs to: _____

Arranged by

Nancy and Randall Faber

Production Coordinator: Jon Ophoff
Cover: Terpstra Design, San Francisco
Engraving: Dovetree Productions, Inc.

FABER
PIANO ADVENTURES®

3042 Creek Drive
Ann Arbor, Michigan 48108

A NOTE TO TEACHERS

ChordTime® Piano Christmas is a collection of favorite Christmas songs arranged for the Level 2B pianist. Both well-known Christmas carols and popular Christmas favorites have been included to provide special appeal to the student.

In addition to being a delightful supplementary book, **ChordTime® Piano Christmas** provides instruction and practice in the use of I, IV, and V⁷ chords. The pieces are arranged in the keys of C, G, and F, with warm-up exercises for each key. The teacher, however, should feel free to skip around among the keys.

ChordTime® Piano Christmas is part of the *ChordTime® Piano* series. "Chord-Time" designates Level 2B of the *PreTime® to BigTime® Piano Supplementary Library* arranged by Faber and Faber.

Following are the levels of the supplementary library, which lead from *PreTime®* to *BigTime®*.

PreTime® Piano	(Primer Level)
PlayTime® Piano	(Level 1)
ShowTime® Piano	(Level 2A)
ChordTime® Piano	(Level 2B)
FunTime® Piano	(Level 3A–3B)
BigTime® Piano	(Level 4)

Each level offers books in a variety of styles, making it possible for the teacher to offer stimulating material for every student. For a complimentary detailed listing, e-mail faber@pianoadventures.com or write us at the mailing address below.

Visit **www.PianoAdventures.com**.

Helpful Hints:

1. The chord warm-ups for a given key should be played daily before practicing the songs.

2. The student can be asked to identify the I, IV, and V⁷ chords in each song and write the correct chord symbol below the bass staff.

3. Hands-alone practice is recommended to facilitate correct fingering and accurate rhythm.

ISBN 978-1-61677-005-1

Copyright © 1988, 2010 by Dovetree Productions, Inc.
c/o FABER PIANO ADVENTURES, 3042 Creek Dr., Ann Arbor, MI 48108

TABLE OF CONTENTS

FF1005

Key of C

Practice these warm-ups before playing the songs in the key of C.

Warm-up 1

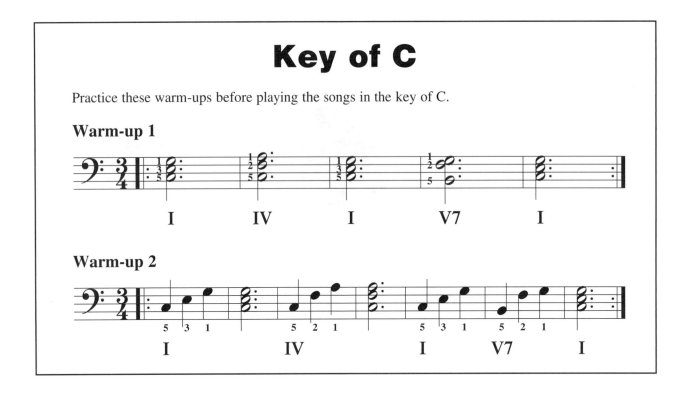

I   IV   I   V7   I

Warm-up 2

I   IV   I   V7   I

Silent Night

Words by JOSEPH MOHR
Music by FRANZ GRÜBER

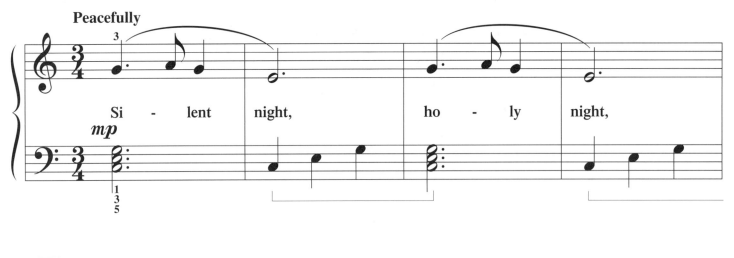

Si - lent night, ho - ly night,

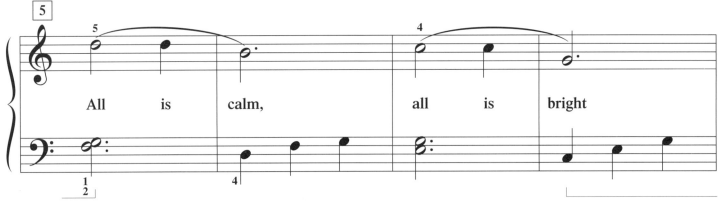

All   is   calm,   all   is   bright

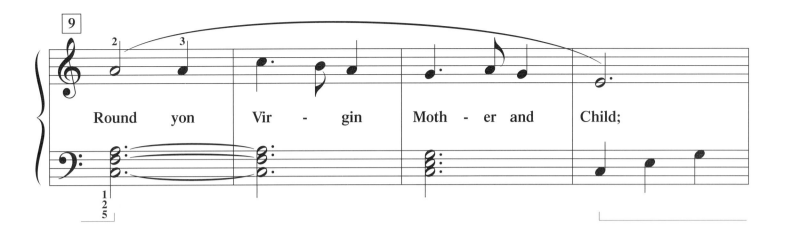

Round yon Vir - gin Moth - er and Child;

Ho - ly In - fant so ten - der and mild,

Sleep in heav - en - ly peace,

mf

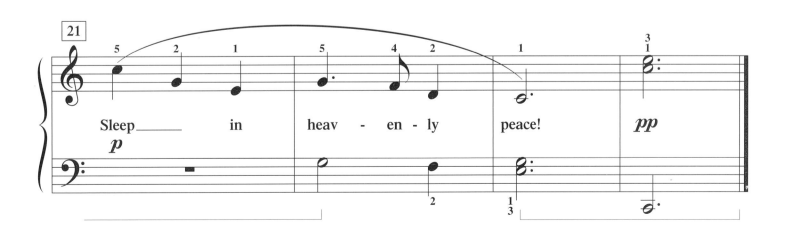

Sleep in heav - en - ly peace!

p *pp*

Joy to the World

Words by ISAAC WATTS
Music by G. F. HÄNDEL

Joy to the world! The Lord is come; Let

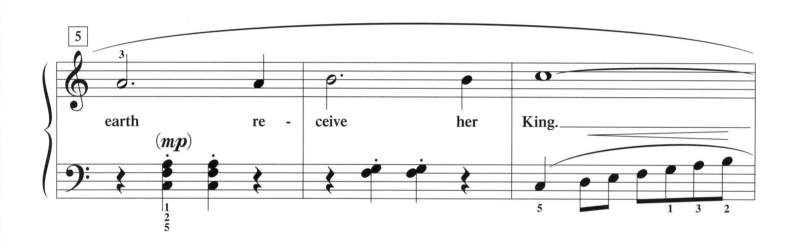

earth re - ceive her King.

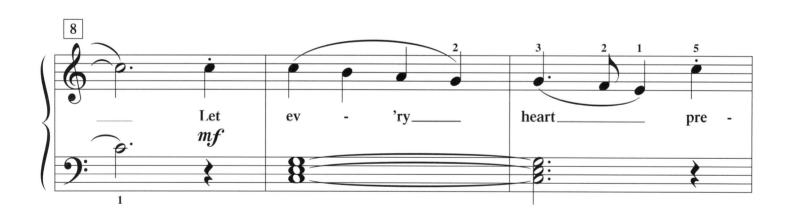

Let ev - 'ry heart pre -

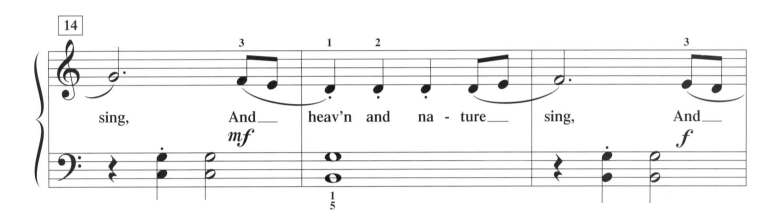

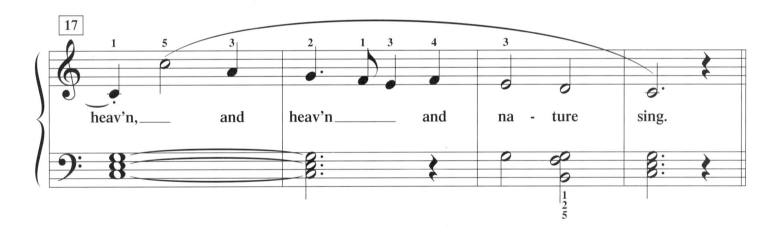

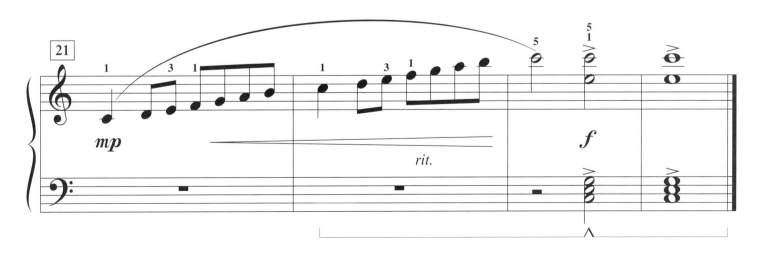

8

Jingle Bells

Words and Music by
J. PIERPONT

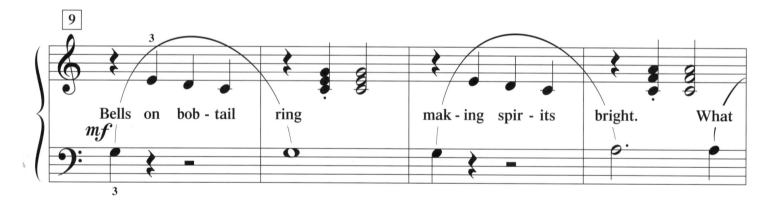

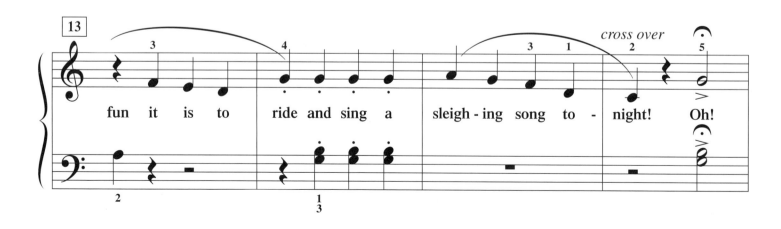

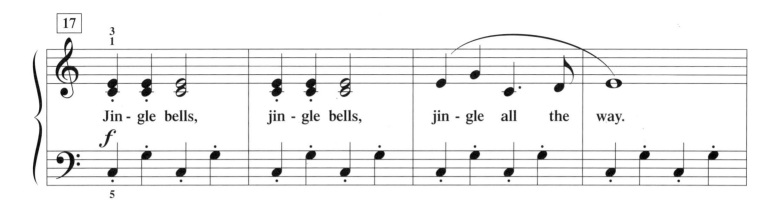

Jin - gle bells, jin - gle bells, jin - gle all the way.

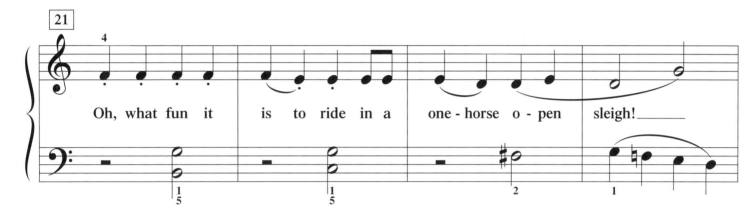

Oh, what fun it is to ride in a one - horse o - pen sleigh!

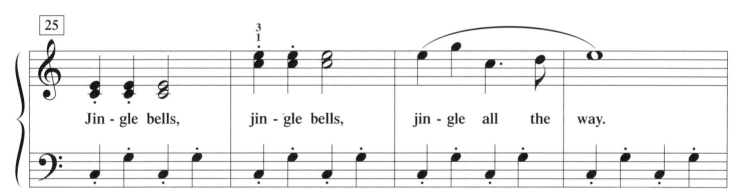

Jin - gle bells, jin - gle bells, jin - gle all the way.

Oh, what fun it is to ride in a one - horse o - pen sleigh!

Optional: Use for an Introduction and an Ending

p　　　　　　　　　　　　　　*rit. (for ending)*

FF1005

When Santa Claus Gets Your Letter

Music and Lyrics by
JOHNNY MARKS

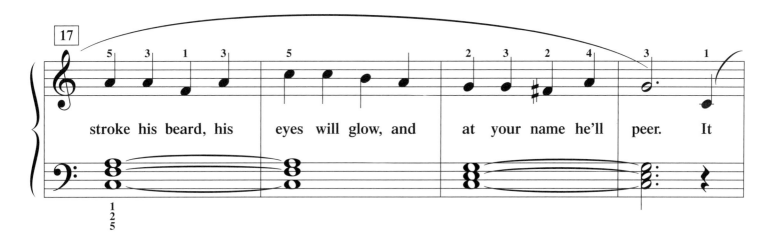

stroke his beard, his eyes will glow, and at your name he'll peer. It

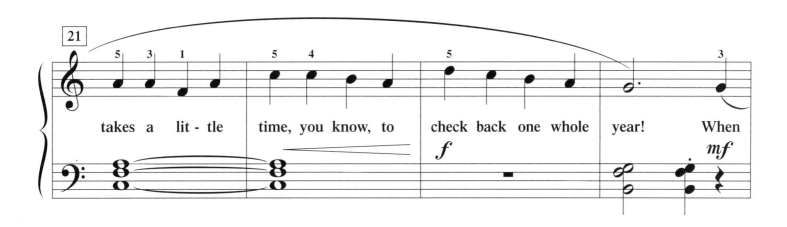

takes a lit - tle time, you know, to check back one whole year! When

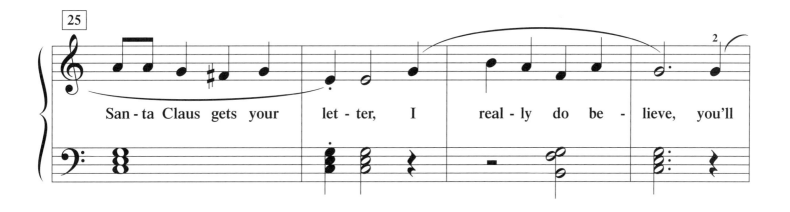

San - ta Claus gets your let - ter, I real - ly do be - lieve, you'll

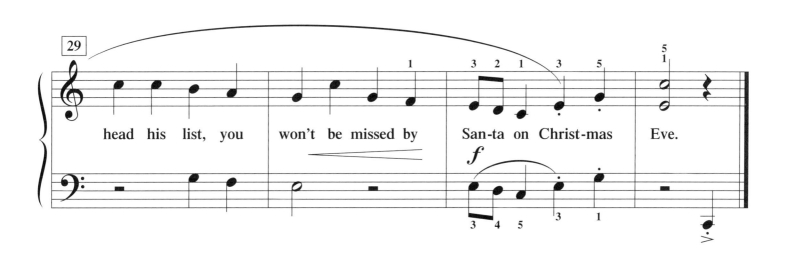

head his list, you won't be missed by San - ta on Christ-mas Eve.

Rockin' Around the Christmas Tree

Music and Lyrics by
JOHNNY MARKS

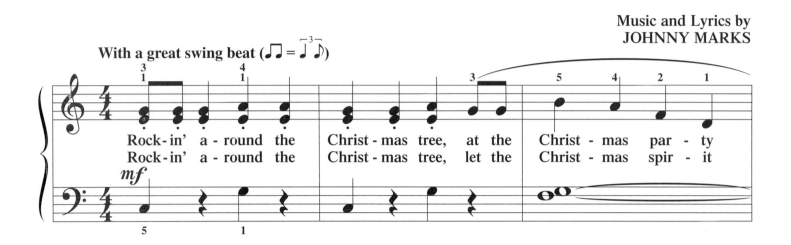

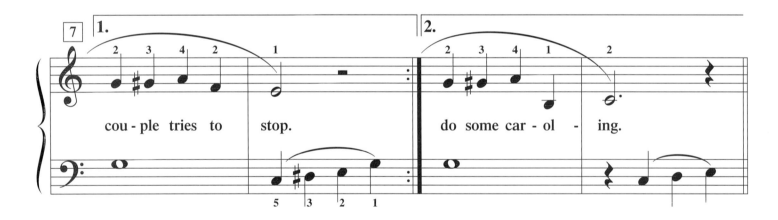

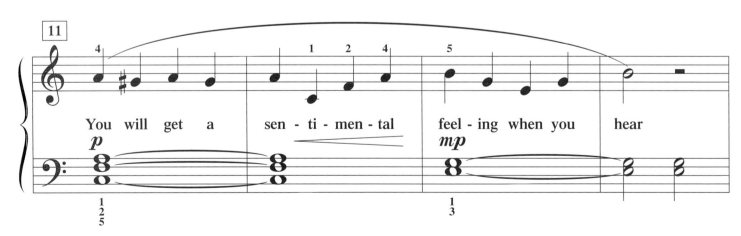

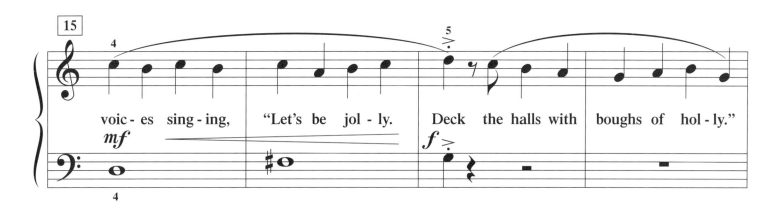

voic - es sing - ing, "Let's be jol - ly. Deck the halls with boughs of hol - ly."

Rock - in' a - round the Christ - mas tree, Have a hap - py hol - i - day.

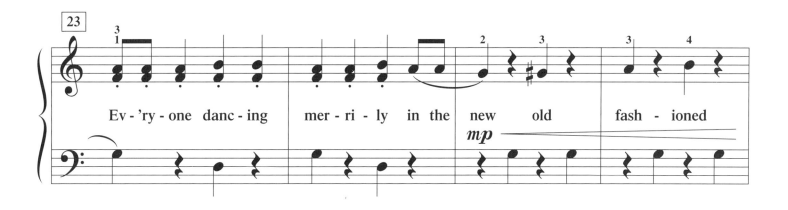

Ev - 'ry - one danc - ing mer - ri - ly in the new old fash - ioned

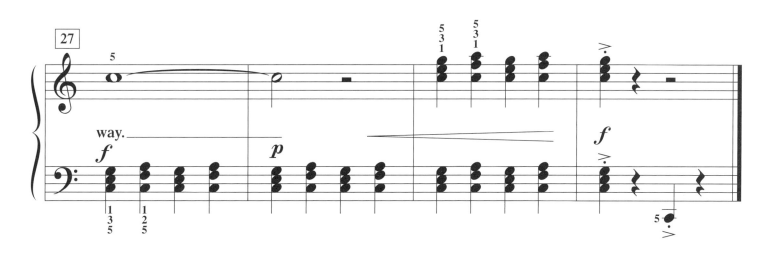

way.

Rudolph the Red-Nosed Reindeer

Music and Lyrics by
JOHNNY MARKS

Ru- dolph, the red-nosed rein-deer had a ver-y shin-y nose.

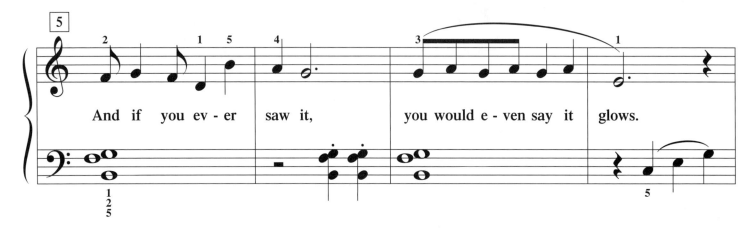

And if you ev- er saw it, you would e - ven say it glows.

All of the oth- er rein-deer used to laugh and call him names,

they nev - er let poor Ru-dolph join in an - y rein-deer games.

15

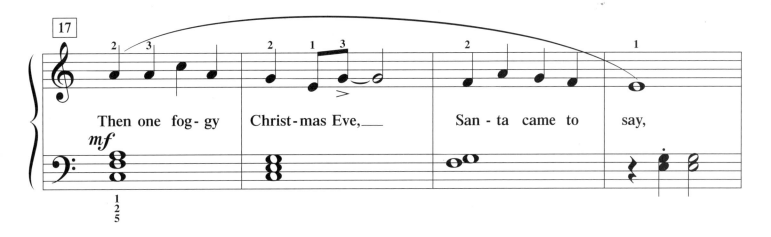

Then one fog-gy Christ-mas Eve,___ San - ta came to say,

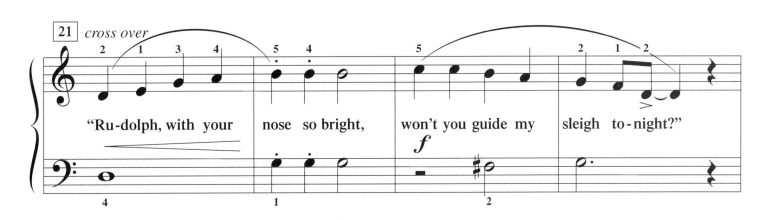

cross over

"Ru-dolph, with your nose so bright, won't you guide my sleigh to-night?"

Then how the rein-deer loved him as they shout-ed out with glee,

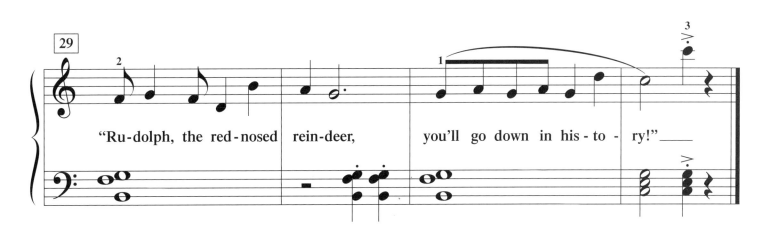

"Ru-dolph, the red-nosed rein-deer, you'll go down in his-to-ry!"___

FF1005

16

The Night Before Christmas Song

Lyrics adapted by JOHNNY MARKS
From Clement Moore's Poem

Music by JOHNNY MARKS

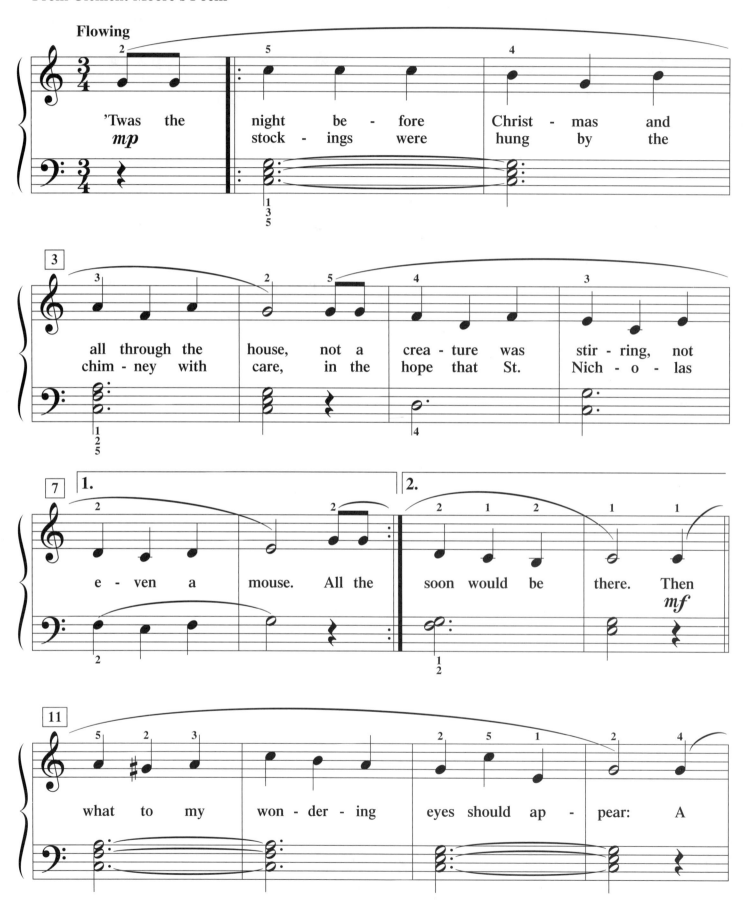

17

FF1005

A Holly Jolly Christmas

Music and Lyrics by
JOHNNY MARKS

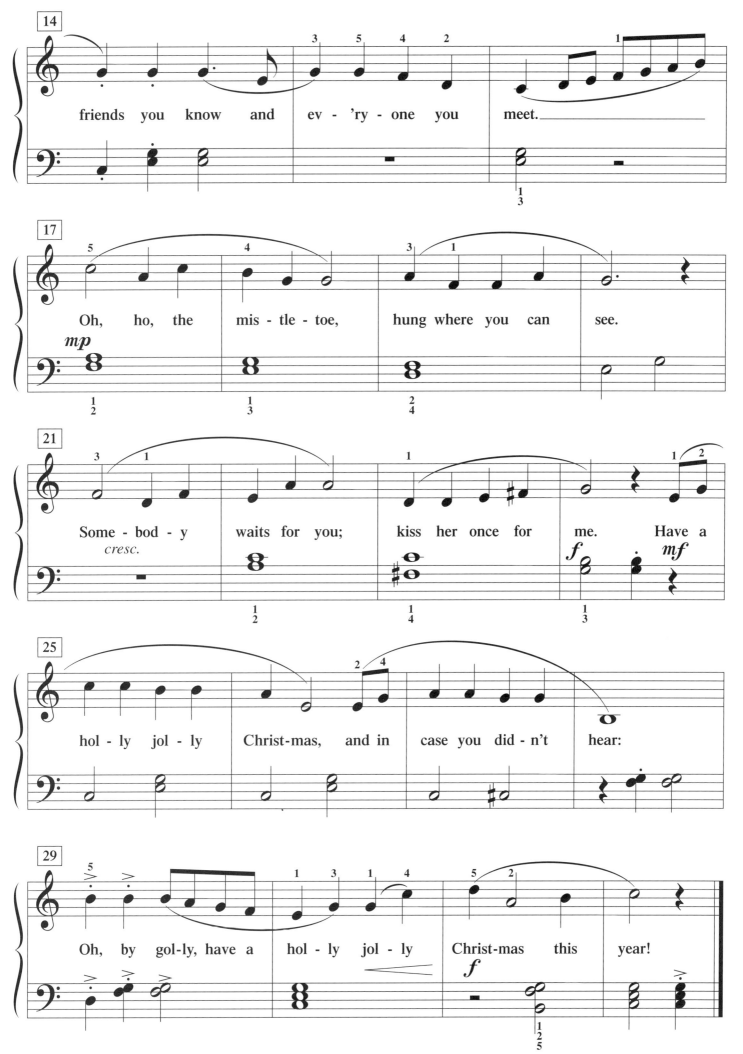

Key of G

Practice these warm-ups before playing the songs in the key of G.

Warm-up 1

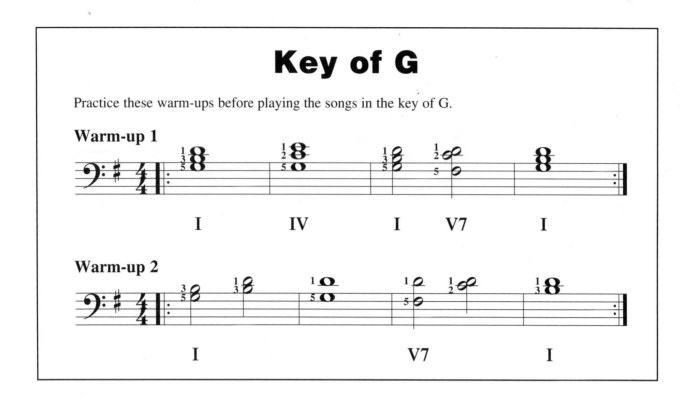

I   IV   I   V7   I

Warm-up 2

I   V7   I

Good King Wenceslas

TRADITIONAL

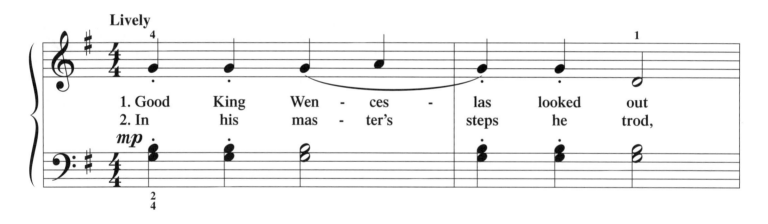

Lively

1. Good King Wen - ces - las looked out
2. In his mas - ter's steps he trod,

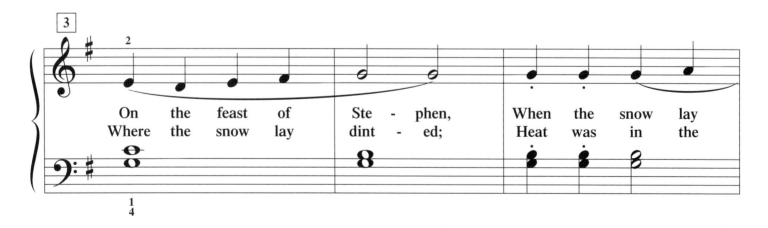

On the feast of Ste - phen,
Where the snow lay dint - ed;

When the snow lay
Heat was in the

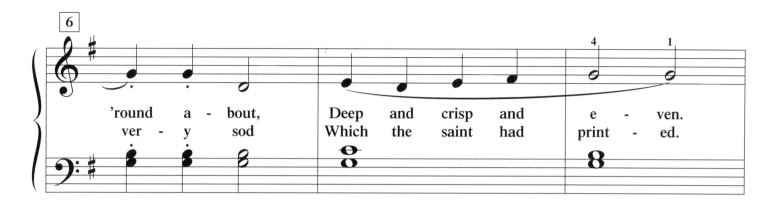

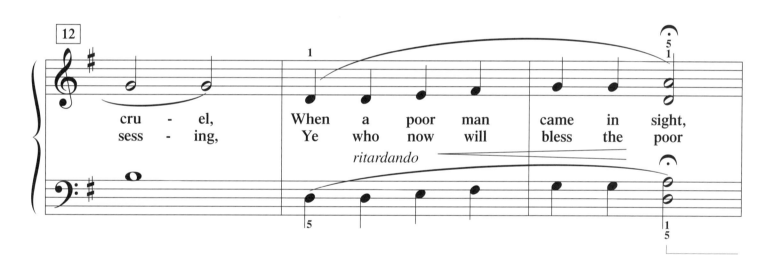

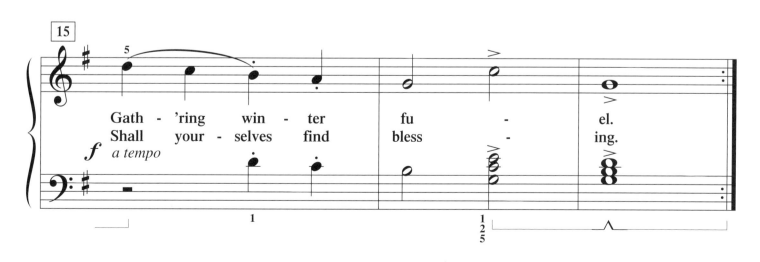

Away in a Manger

Music by JAMES R. MURRAY
Words ANON. LUTHERAN

Jolly Old Saint Nicholas

TRADITIONAL

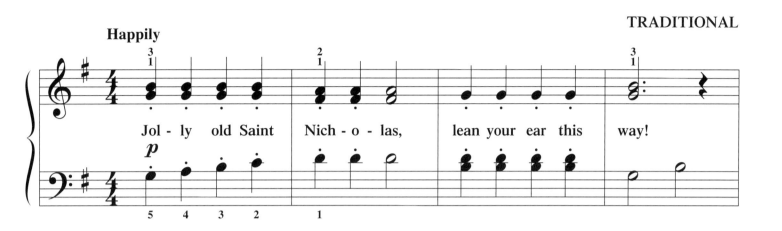

Jol - ly old Saint Nich - o - las, lean your ear this way!

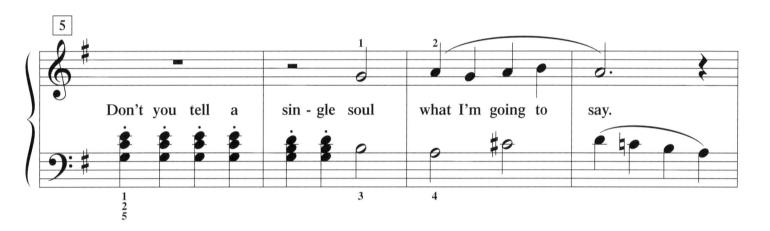

Don't you tell a sin - gle soul what I'm going to say.

Christ - mas Eve is com - ing soon. Now, you dear old man,

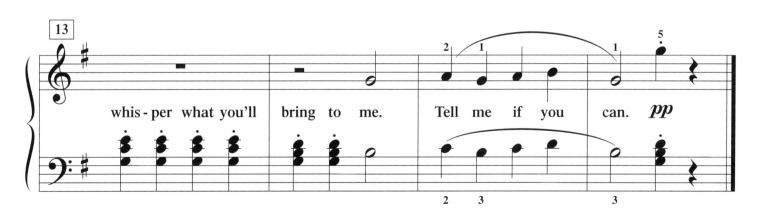

whis - per what you'll bring to me. Tell me if you can.

Key of F

Practice these warm-ups before playing the songs in the key of F.

Warm-up 1

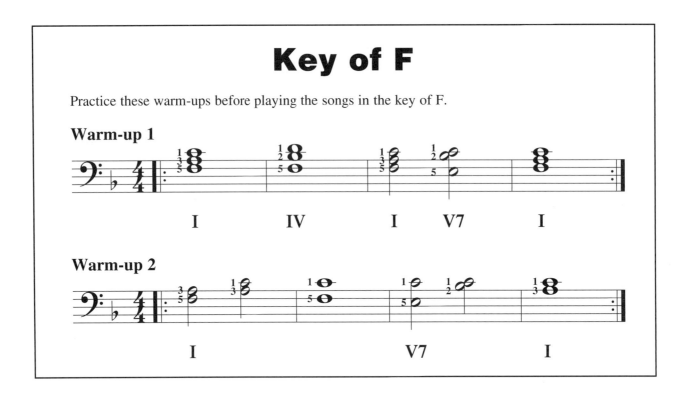

Warm-up 2

Deck the Halls

TRADITIONAL

With excitement

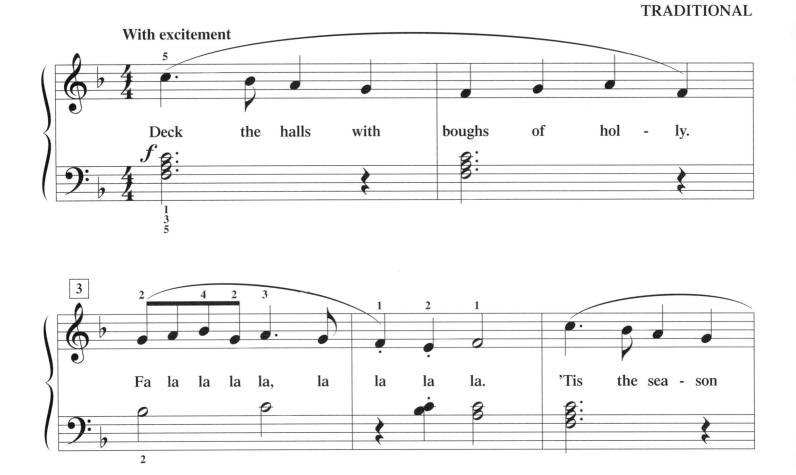

Deck the halls with boughs of hol - ly.

Fa la la la la, la la la la. 'Tis the sea - son

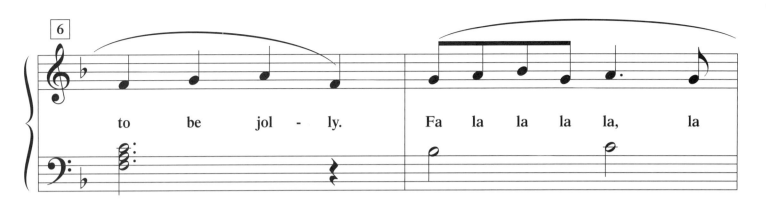

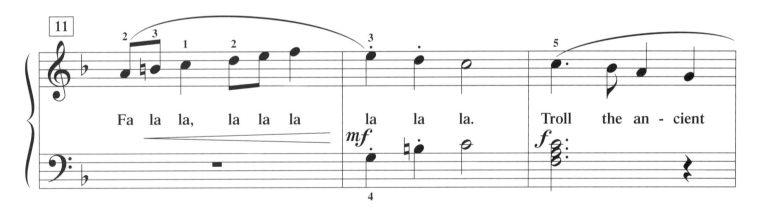

The Twelve Days of Christmas

TRADITIONAL

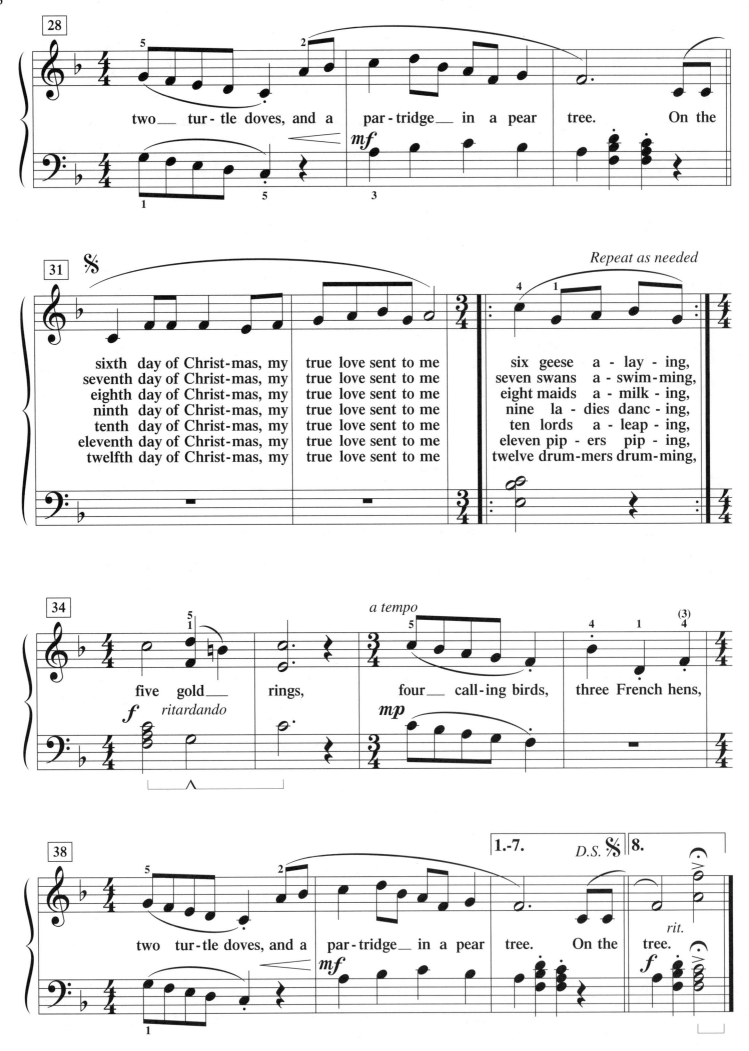